20 Day Online Classroom Team Building Challenge

Silly Yet Effective Virtual Activities to Build Trust Quickly and Make Your Class More Engaging Than Ever!

Publisher's Note

The publication is designed to provide accurate and authoritative information regarding the subject matter covered. It is sold with the understanding that the publisher is not engaged in rendering psychological, financial, legal, or other professional services. If expert assistance or counseling is needed, the services of a competent professional should be sought.

For Bowen,

my extraordinary partner in life and work

Table of Contents

Why This Book?

Are you looking for ways to better connect with your learners when everyone only sees each other through a flat-screen? Do you want to turn this current virtual classroom challenge into an opportunity to build a stronger sense of community?

So, you start to search on the internet:

online/remote learning activities
online class team building
distance learning playbook
fun distance learning activities

If that sounds like you, then search no further.

How can this book help me?

This little distance learning playbook is here to help you. You will learn 20 silly yet engaging virtual activities. So you can get your virtual classroom to laugh more, interact more, engage more, and have even more fun as though you were all still in a physical classroom!

The first part will get your class to have some quick laughs. The second part gets into more sophisticated online class team building activities that may require some preparation. Still, it will definitely hype up the engagement and get the learning going. You will learn everything necessary to transform your virtual classroom from "good" to "excellent."

I know as educators, we are all swamped, especially at this time. But no matter how busy you are, you will always find those activities easy to do and funny to play just through your screen!

What are some sample activities?

- Virtual scavenger hunt
- Experts in the show
- 1 plus 2
- Threads of fun
- Virtual Tap
- One Thing

Is this book for me?

This book is designed with all educators and trainers in mind (Pre-K, K-12, higher education, or corporate training). This book is a must-read if you want to have more engaging learning experiences with your students and trainees in the virtual classrooms. Let's make it happen now!

Chapter 1: Everything Goes Online!

At the beginning of 2020, many colleges and schools around the world closed because of COVID-19. Many students, professors, and faculty members had to learn how to teach online in a big rush as the whole world moved online so fast. Since then, many books have been written about how teachers need to adapt to teach online classes and play with all types of technologies involved with online courses. How can we set up online meetings? What are the requirements for our devices? How to prepare assignments just as before? Or, just like what you are interested in, how can we effectively engage students in this type of environment? I know all of these make students feel anxious, but we still have to work things out and make it happen in our online classroom.

This is from a teacher:

"It just changed so fast, fast that I almost feel my work and things around me are not the way they were before. My college was shut down, and we were asked to bring everything up online. We were trained and educated on preparing stuff, teaching, and teamwork online, but things were just different again. Even though I've known how to prepare for it, engage students, and arrange my works, I still feel we have missed many things, and it's a different feeling. Yes, we are still getting up early to prepare and have classes, students are still learning as much as possible, but these are very new. While we are still adapting to so many things, we are just not relaxed and don't have enough fun like how we did before, we work hard and not sure what else can we do about it."

And this is from a student:

"The world has changed, and last month our professor announced we need to go back home, and they will figure out how we can carry things on for the rest of this semester. I was just anxious and wondered many things at that time: is this the end of this semester? What about my projects in the lab? And what do I do with my part-time job in the Mall? I guess we are still lucky that we transferred everything online, and we are trying to adapt to this. However, my anxiety and pressure are still here. I can no longer catch up with my friends or get to the class earlier and chat around with professor Lee. On the one hand, it's just weird to see everyone just on the tiny screen. You can only access materials through the small window. On the other hand, I feel we are not that chilled and don't have enough time to catch up and play. Still, just chasing the schedule and jumping from one meeting to the other one, it just not good enough, I guess."

Yes, teaching and learning remotely do have some downsides. Students in virtual classrooms may feel lonely, anxious to adapt to new environments, and bothered by tight schedules. Teachers are struggling with all sorts of schedules and new technologies. They find it's challenging to prepare materials, arrange schedules, and even hit the timeline they used to do. So being stressed, both teachers and students are just trying very hard in the virtual classroom. They are not interacting with each other as they would in a regular classroom. Meetings, group discussions, in particular, were often very awkward and dry because it's hard to teamwork and share things as how we could do it as before. That is one significant downside to virtual classrooms— the lack of time for fun. Students were used to going to school earlier and chatting about things that are not related to the class, as the schedule for the upcoming weekend, showing each other some funny stuff, and even gathering together to check out their new phone' earbuds. And during the class, not only do teachers feel weird about online interactions, but students also can't manage to reach out to their neighbors to catch up with the last topics, share their notes, and catch up during the break to talk about something they feel curious or exciting. Although such small and random interactions may seem trivial and unnecessary, their impact on classroom performances is significant for both students and teachers. So, teachers should develop some activities and encourage students to participate. And that will help realize these class-bonding moments to enhance their connection and classroom performances and promote their learning, as virtual classrooms need this more than ever.

Chapter 2: Manage Your Online Classroom

Be the expert of everyone.

If you've ever had the experience of hearing someone remember the little detail you've shared about yourself in the past, you know how good it makes you feel, right? And imagine you hear that from your teacher or professor! You will be impressed by that and even change how you think of him!

Although not everyone is interested in sharing their personal life (and it's important to respect that), most students appreciate it when you take the time to learn about them. During the class break, most students love to chat around and share information such as preferred names, nicknames, exciting stories of their pets, children's names, birthdays, holidays, and more. Many of them still do the same thing in an online classroom. Even if you are just sitting there, listening to their conversations, you can also learn something. Like their favorite local restaurants, snacks/sweets that they love most, and class activities. Thus it's fun and essential to hear your students share about things like those. More importantly, as we said before, this online learning environment is very new and make students stress out, so it's not easy for them to sit back and relax. So as their teacher, you need to create a safe space to relax and share their stuff. It works even if you just sit there, listen to their conversations, and occasionally get into the conversation. It's essential to get to know your students for a better teacher-student connection.

Cultures and backgrounds

Do you ever teach students of other cultures? or do some of them (even yourself) live in a different part of the world? If so, it's essential to show your respect to them by learning about their cultures. If applicable, always learning about them by asking things like:

- What do you want students in my culture/country to understand about interacting with you?
- What are the stupid mistakes that aliens often make when they visit/work in your country?

Other than that, do your homework and be aware of their local holidays and traditions. Put it in your calendar, and give your students some surprises if you would like to. This is a great way to make closer connections and strengthen the chemical reaction within your students. It means a lot to students when they feel that you know and care about how they think and feel, especially in such an environment when there might be many anxious hearts out there.

Life out of the classroom

One of the simplest and often overlooked ways to show remote students your respect is caring and valuing their time. As the classroom leader, many of us tend to accidentally burn some bridges. We often tend to "borrow another five minutes" after the bell rings. Or send another assignment for them to preview on weekends, especially now when our schedule is delayed because we haven't fully got used to online teaching. I believe we are all responsible educators and are available seven days a week, but that doesn't mean all our students are. Teachers who respect their students' time and personal lives often more quickly win the whole class's trust and respect. And understanding availabilities have also required some homework to be done by us. Things that need to be learned are as below:

- Do your students have part-time jobs or take other classes that require them to pay extra attention and spend extra hours?
- Do your students have any family issues or other responsibilities that take the rest of their time?
- What are the time zones of your students if you are teaching some international students?

Thank you

"How long does it take for a teacher to reach out when a student who has done something wrong in his assignment?"

In about a minute.

"OK, then how long does it take for the teacher to get in touch with a student who did something excellent in his project?"

Perhaps never, for some of us.

Whether your students are passionate about your class or not, they are glad to know that whatever they did well will be appraised. Here are a few simple ways to show students your appreciation for their excellent performances:

- When everyone joins the class, appraise the student and state why you are appraising him and what he did to earn it.
- When you have finished grading for their assignments, if you see someone has made significant progress, or excellently accomplished a task, email your students or announce that in blackboard, let them know what they accomplished should be promoted.

Always be there for them.

Among all the successful educators and instructors that I have ever seen in my career, there is one obvious thing which they all have in common: they are all made available to their students at all levels whenever their students need them. Whether how bust they are, these educators understand that one of the most valuable things they could offer to their students is not always their knowledge and approaches but also their time, encouragement, and support. As the teacher, the most efficient way to motivate and engage your students is by showing them that you are here available to support them.

Here are several ways to show your class that you are available:

- Let them know the best times to reach you and the best ways to get to you before and after class so they can keep in mind.

- Provide ways to reach out to you through Email, WhatsApp, Slack, and others if you are comfortable with it.
- Chat with your students about what level of communication works the best for them, and see if they need help from you outside the classroom.

Help your students grow.

One of the best ways to respect students and show their value is to measure their academic and career growth. You can achieve this by discussing and asking about their important educational or personal goals, in their points of view, and then finding ways to support them in achieving those goals. Here are some ways you can think about to help them:

- Provide regular feedback about their progress based on their performances in and off class, and give them time to ask questions.

- Let them know about some training, upcoming conferences, and other useful materials to motivate them to learn better.

- Help them connect to other internal and external professors and educators in your field if they show some interest in specific areas.

- Work with them to work out their confusion to help them meet their goals.

Treat everyone in trust.

Trust is the most important topic in learning and teaching remotely. While it is important to trust your students, students also need to trust you for a better teacher-student connection. Many of us have been working in organizations where trust is not paid attention by others, and it sucks. Teachers are too stressed out and always be suspicious that their students might be chatting through their phones or even watching Netflix when the class is going on. This assumption always leads to an uncomfortable learning experience, unhappy and stressed students, and bad outcomes. It is up to you as an instructor to avoid this by fostering trust between you and them.

Trust is particularly critical when building a culture in a remote environment, especially since all of you are not seeing each other at this moment. But no matter how the situation is, once trust is planted into your classroom, it will motivate us to work through obstacles and any problems that occur together, which will boost their learning experience and cultivate a growth mindset in your classroom.

When things get tough

We don't like it, but sometimes hard conversations are necessary, especially in education, to make greater progress. When you're in the argument with your students, like arguing about their performance, the timeline of a project, or other things, it's easy to forget that, besides the outcomes, more importantly, you want them to grow, you want to encourage them to be better, and you want to improve the relationship with them at the end of the day. So we need to approach arguments to protect that as a NO.1 priority, not just to address the problem and walk away to leave your students with an empty head.

One of the techniques is the concept of "making it safe." The idea is that you need to create the right conditions for a tough conversation by establishing mutual respect in between. It's tough under the situation of learning from home because being virtual means that our intentions can be misunderstood in the wrong mood and at the wrong time. You can't see body language and other non-verbal signals via phone call or email. In fact, research has shown that most students cannot recognize the tongue of others in emails. They just don't get the emotion in it. So the best approach here is not sending another ten emails to explain where you are getting to. Just take the time to make a phone or video call to make sure it's all right. Check the temperature of the person to make sure something you said wasn't bothering them. All it takes is to pick up a phone and communicate, person to person, in the working environment.

Always getting feedback

We can't make any more significant progress without feedback — otherwise, you will get out of the way and not be sure what is correct and what could be better. Regular feedback is particularly critical for all of us, learning and teaching virtually. When we are having limited physical interactions now, you need to take extra steps to get feedback and understand how students feel about you, the approaches you take in the class, and the whole learning experience in general, to help them make more progress in this journey, and to make sure you are all on the same page. You can't purely rely on chats in front of the camera to find out what's going on behind the screen. Consider how much feedback comes out of class in your life. We're used to rating every great product online when purchasing something, judging both the good and the bad, and contributing to a vast data pool that helps the retailers improve. Why should this be any different when it comes to us as educators? You can include questions like below:

- "What three things can I do to improve? And for what aspects?"
- "Was there anything we haven't discussed that could have been done to positively affect your experience here?"
- How's the learning experience you have when you take my class?
- Or you may even discuss specific approaches that you took with your students and see how they feel about that.

Chapter 3: From Good to Excellent

Connection before and during the class

Have you ever seen someone come up to ask for something without even saying hello to you? If so, you would probably feel he or she was rude. It's essential to start every class or call by taking a minute to connect before you jump to the content (yes, I know we have tight schedules, but this is important). A good rule of thumb is to spend the first 5 minutes on interactions with your students to connect to the content afterward.

Also, for a balanced and well-connected virtual class, I recommend that for every hour you spend on the course, take out five or ten minutes to build relationships. You could spend five minutes at the beginning of the class and five minutes at the end of the course to wrap it up. If you've got a 2-hour conference or presentation, give them a stretch break or play a quick game, which we will get to afterward.

Make varieties & surprises.

The whole purpose of creating this book is to give you a simple way to add a little variety and fun to your remote interactions. Keep your students tuned in and out of their toes by surprising them with a mix of activities. That can be realized by adding some questions, challenges, learning, and surprises, just like adding different flavors to your ice cream. Each time, it will give you some surprises.

Be consistent and create rituals.

Although it may seem contradictory to the one I just talked about, it is also important to develop consistent]practices and rituals in the middle of all varieties and surprises. If students know you're going to start the course by asking them to share a recent accomplishment, an exciting life story, or just a review of the previous class, they're going to be excited to take your class and get ready to talk each time they jump on the screen. They know when they'll have time to talk, share, and learn to enjoy the content as you are doing this each time, which will benefit the whole group that they will know what's the right time for what, just to make sure to add some surprises here so most of them will have fun and look forward to it each time, and on the other hand, will improve the quality of their learning experiences.

Be a builder of the classroom culture.

A team or group can maintain a great culture because of those team members who protect and promote culture and help develop the culture over time. You can enhance your value in the big community by acting as the culture builder, especially if you are the educator and the classroom leader. When a great educator leads the class teaching the culture in the classroom, they always make sure that everyone realizes that they are now the protectors of our culture. Once they understand the culture, they have an equal responsibility to keep healthy, thus enhancing each other's connection.

Chapter 4: Warm Up

Manage the time

When you've planned an activity for 10 minutes in one of your classes, it's a must to follow that just to make sure it is working as you said. When you find the time is running out and not everyone has participated, that's cool. You can do a few things to move forward:

- Ask them if they want to keep going for 5 more minutes and ask students to be concise with their responses.

- Schedule the operation and pick up where you left off at the next class when you have time to do it.

- Or, when the bell rings, just stop the action.

How you want students to participate

After you've introduced an activity, describing how you want your students to participate. Just like if you're asking a question, start by answering it yourself. If you want them to be concise and cut to the point, give yours a brief response. If you want them to provide more details, then share more information of yours. Students prefer to learn and follow the reaction of the first person who just left as a standard.

If you're hosting a more profound activity that requires your students to think about a question or prepare before you get started, save some time by sending the information to them in advance.

Keep the conversation going.

If this is something, you had never done before. Students didn't respond immediately when you tried an activity in one of your classes, don't worry. Next time just call them up to jumpstart some discussions and expressions. Keeping the conversation going is healthy because that gives all students opportunities to talk about points of view from themselves, ask questions, and know more about each other.

The Bowl of Name

One of the funniest games I ever played with my class before was to place a bowl or a bag on your desk with all our students' names on tiny pieces of paper. You can throw the bag up and down on your desk to randomly choose a person to answer questions or get involved in other activities. And then, take those names out of the bowl, who have already participated until you've worked through everybody, and feel free to start this process again. That way, they're all going to be picked up at this round, and make sure you introduce this before you get started, so everyone is aware of and agrees with it.

Day 1: Question of the Day

Time requirement: 10 minutes or less

The first activity here is to help your students get to know each other better by starting each of your class with a day's question. Select one of the items below or think out something else if you think it will be more enjoyable. Also, give them a few minutes to react and answer the question, chat about how they feel about it, and even share some jokes about it. I'm sure this will make the meeting way more energetic than it used to be.

Here are the questions for you to select. Feel free to add more if you like:

- What is one simple fact about each of you? (this will be a good hint for activity 2)
- If you could click a button and one task on your to-do list would be automatically completed, what would it be and why?
- What made you happy last week?
- Who would you like to hang out with?
- (If you have college students) Who is still single?
- What's the biggest lie you ever told?
- What would you do as the last thing if tomorrow is the end of the world?
- What was the strangest thing you've ever done?

- What movie did you watch more than five times? How about video games?
- What was your favorite person in the class?
- What kind of food do you eat most when you're stressed?
- What's the strangest food you've ever eaten?

A bonus activity

Time: 10 Minutes (prepared-1 Hour)

Preparation – Interview your class.

Make a short online survey (Survey Monkey works excellent) with each student's name and a text box. Have everyone take the study and write 3-5 words to describe each other. After that, use words written about each of them in the survey to create a word cloud for them. Share the story cloud at your next virtual class via share screen, and let them try and guess who each cloud represents. After that, give them their word clouds.

Day 2: Guess Who

Time requirement: 5 minutes per student in total

Resources needed: an Excel spreadsheet.

Facts	Guesses from <Name 1>	Guesses from <Name 2>	Guesses from <Name 3>	Correct Answer [Note: Hide this column and do not reveal until the end of the game]
Fact 1				
Fact 2				
Fact 3				
Fact 4				
Fact 5				
Fact 6				
Fact 7				
Fact 8				
Total Correct and Scores				

Summary of rules:
- Everyone submitted a fun fact about themselves to you through email.
- You will share a spreadsheet of all those facts, and all students will have to guess who's the person that each fact belongs to
- If one of those facts is yours. You may choose to guess your own fact correctly or let someone else guess

- The student who had the most amount of correct guesses wins.
- Maybe some small gifts can be used as a prize.

The goal of this game is to let you interact with your students on a personal level. Normally, virtual classmates don't have lots of chances to interact or talk to each other in a day, as they used to in the physical classroom, so this game is perfect for that reason because your students can open up to each other and learn about everyone's background and funny stories if some of them they don't know a lot about each other before.

Here is how it works.

To start with, ask each one to give you three personal facts about them as a facilitator. They usually will be conservative initially, but later on, there will be some wild and weird ones, so you still have to filter them. Just make sure they're giving you things that will make the rest of the team hard to guess. If you have a big class, you'll need to ask each person for just one fact, so things can be controlled well, and the game doesn't take a lot of time.

Everyone in the class will need to email you their information privately a few days before the class going on so that you have enough time to filter the details. You will then type those into the spreadsheet you have.

On the day of the class you want to host this activity, you will then share this spreadsheet via a screen (If you are using software like Webex, Zoom, or Team, etc.) and ask each student to guess who this is. You'll start with "Fact 1" on the top of the sheet by reading it loudly and asking each of the students to guess who they think this is. Then next to "Fact 1", type in their guesses and names, from left to right on the same row, with "Guesses from <Name xxx>" on the top of the spreadsheet. Make sure to keep displaying your computer so that everyone can see them. Once that row is done, move to the next row for "Fact 2", repeat for the rest of the facts, and not reveal the correct answers yet until the game is over.

Remember that each student can "guess" his or her own facts. They can either be honest about it, or they can pick someone else to guess. Which makes it even more fun and competitive.

Once you have filled in all the guesses from everyone, you can show the correct answers of them within the same row, on the very right side of the screen (if you don't know how to hide the answers, just type them in one by one, so they will see it in order). And when you go through the right answers, give them some time to talk about them, add up the total number of correct answers under each name, which are scores of each one, and put them at the bottom of the sheet. You can even offer some incentives and small gifts to the student who won the highest score.

Make sure you actually try this one when you have time. This activity is a lot more interesting than it sounds. When you actually play with your students, if the facts are really ridiculous, their guesses are going to be insane as well! And the facts you find out would reveal quite a lot about each student's background, which can be a fun part of your culture in the long run.

Try this simple one out too.

Time Needed: Approximately. 10 minutes

This game aims to have a few laughs with your students during the sparing time and keep everyone up. It also encourages everyone to think about some funny and smart answers.

At the beginning of your class, play the standard "caption this" game by sharing an image and asking your students to develop a caption for it. (If you have never played this before, just Google the traditional version of caption this)

Make sure you don't share a photo with someone before the class so that no one can think and prepare for ideas ahead of the activity.

When it begins, post the picture through screen-sharing, and give everyone 50 seconds to think about the caption. Then let them send it to you privately (via chat or email).

Once they have sent in their answers, enter them in a spreadsheet (don't show your students yet) with your students' names.

When you have finished, cover up the name column, and post the spreadsheet to the class so that anyone can read through the captions. Then ask everyone to vote for the funniest one.

After you tally up all the votes, you will "unhide" the column to announce the winner's name, who just got the most votes. It's also important to remind everyone to keep their responses clean.. You may also let them know that you have the right to reject their answers, which are too insulting or inappropriate, and ask them to change privately.

Have you ever?

With a few tweaks, this party game can be a funnier way to make your virtual class laugh. If you've never played "Have You ever" before, it's pretty easy. One student asks the rest of the class a question like, for example, "Have you ever faked a lousy signal to get yourself off an online course? All the students who have ever done this must raise their hands in front of the camera!

It's better if some students can come up with their own questions, but here are a few to get you started:

- Have you ever gone to the bathroom when you were on a call?
- Have you ever bragged in front of others that you got a full score?
- Have you stacked stuff under your desk to make them out of reach to look like your office was cleaner than it was?
- Have you ever forgotten a classroom before you were called by the professor?

- Have you ever fallen asleep while others were talking?
- Have you ever watched a full show on YouTube or Netflix while on a call?
- Have you ever been to a restaurant without a wallet, so you had to call your friends to rescue you?

Tip: You can make this more visual by allowing students to turn off their cameras and then turn them back on if they did that: "Hey, look! Mike went dark on this one again!!"

Day 3: Virtual Scavenger Hunt

Time required: 10 minutes or less.

Resources needed: items in the house (portable and not bulky)

Another exciting activity that you can do is to organize a quick-fire scavenger hunt. Before playing this game, get your students to brainstorm and develop up to 30 things (also, you can use the list below for ideas). Then you can pick 6-10 items from these 30 things (in case someone prepares for this on purpose) and tell all of them that you're going to run this at some random meetings. You'll mention one of the things on the list randomly and see who's the fastest one to get back to their computer with it.

Possible items you can choose from:

- Parts of some sports facilities
- Your dad's wallet
- Your raincoat
- A photo of your childhood
- Your old phones
- Your toothbrush and a newspaper
- A dumpster
- Some coins from a different country
- A glass full of water

Tip: It's best to pick something that will trigger a conversation and guesses behind it. When they take that back, ask them to give a one-minute description of the object and the story behind it. If someone didn't

have it, they need to comment on each of them the rest
of the students brought back.

Day 4: Experts in the Show

Time requirement: 5 minutes for each of them

Summary of rules:

- You're going to pose a question to the class that you don't have any idea about
- One cover slide shows the topic is written, plus five separate slides with topic-related images.
- Each of the five slides has one image.
- Each student will present the subject with a straight and serious face as they are an "expert" about it without laughing.
- Start with the introduction of the topic, and then show the slides.
- After around 20 seconds or once the student finishes, you will hear some feedback from the rest of the class, then switch to the next topic and repeat the process.

This game aims to let everyone laugh a few times as one of them practices his improvisation skills. This is useful, especially after some intense assignments or exams.

This is how it works.

As the host, you should prepare a set of slides ahead of time on several random topics (preferably ridiculous topics). For each topic, you will need to pair 5 slides along with that (and do not share them with anyone in the class, to make the most out of the game).

During the activity, you can select a participant for the 1st topic, tell them about the 1st topic, and then present the 1st slide with the topic written to give the participant the idea and get ready. Next, present the rest of 5 slides in front of everyone.

The participant needs to pretend to be a global expert on the subject and improvises for five minutes as they go through the slides trying the best to hold their face straight. As we talked before, the topics can be something dumb and ridiculous. The slides are also silly but related to the topic. The more random and funny the slides are, the more fun the presentation will be.

For example, you can pick a topic called "how to be adorable" and prepare some slides, including pictures of infants, jellyfish, and even caterpillars (just make it ridiculous but are still related to the topic). The participant must present with a straight face till the end of the last slide and may ask you to switch to the next slide when they can't do it anymore (you can think of some punishments for that, just for fun). You also have the option to switch to the next slide whenever you feel it's good to move on.

This game is not only entertaining, but it also helps students develop their online and public speaking skills and how to handle things that they found embarrassing.

Day 5: Surprise!

Time requirement per game: 20 minutes or less

Game 1

Let everyone in the class pick a small item like a little doll, coffee cup, or a book they have at home. Before each play, let them move the object to a different location within the camera's view. See who's able to see the change. Another version is to get students to turn off their cameras for 30 seconds and change one thing in their room. After that, turn the camera back on, ask students to guess what has changed!

Game 2

This is a simple game for your virtual class to have a little fun to play at your next course. Let one of your students pick a famous person, whether alive or dead. Next, let others ask questions that you can answer with "yes" or "no" until they have enough information to guess who they are. Sample questions as below:

Is he or she still alive? No

Is he or she an artist, huh? Yes, yes.

Did he or she die in the last 10 years? Yes, yes.

Is he or she a kid, huh? Yes, yes.

Is he or she a country singer, huh? No

Game 3

It's hard to have a smooth video call without a freeze on someone's phone, especially if you have a big class to teach. But it will be so much fun if you turn that into a game by trying to trick each other into believing that you're frozen. Pick a random time to do this with your students (just like when you have finished your class, and just try to do something relaxing one day, or at a lunch break) without telling them until you stop moving and pretend to be frozen. When someone says, "Looks like our professor is frozen," that's a win for you! Did your colleague's computer freeze in the middle of a meeting sometimes? Sounds funny right? You can take a screenshot or a video to keep a memory of the best awkward freezes!

Game 4

Have you ever had a hard time getting some of your students to show up on your phone calls or class right on time? If it's not because of some severe problems or personal issues, try to make a game out of it. The last one showing up on the screen has to answer 5 random questions in front of the whole class. Choose some items as below. Keep it fun and ridiculous. Remember that someone might be late for your class because of their lifestyles or personal schedules, don't make it a burden. Always use activities to cheer them up!

- Have you ever stopped paying attention and then got asked a question from your teachers and had to fake your answer to satisfy him or her?

- Have you ever attended an online conference but forgot to have pants on?
- Have you ever forgotten a call completely until anyone else called you?
- Have you ever fallen asleep while others were talking or during a class?
- Have you ever lied about having a wrong signal to not using video because you were somewhere you were not supposed to be?
- Have you ever watched a TV show or played a video game while on a call, so you had to mute yourself?

Bonus activity time!

Time Required: Approximately. 2 minutes for each student.

This activity aims to have your students list up to three of their pet peeves and speak to the whole class about them as an exciting activity to wrap up the class at the end of the day.

Peeves are objects that students find incredibly frustrating and something that they find irritating to them—the stranger the pet peeves and the funnier the game.

One of my pet peeves, for example, sees an ice cream left outside the fridge for more than two minutes. The feeling of ice cream melting at the table just drives me crazy, well, this is a boring one, but I think you guys will have more funny ones.

Sharing these types of pet peeves will make you laugh a few times, and you'll learn more about your students' personalities in this way, more or less.

Here are a few other examples I gathered when I asked students to share the following:

- Squeezing the toothpaste tube from the middle
- Filling the dishwasher in the wrong way
- Listening to students chewing at the table

Your students can also share slides with images of their pet peeves, but limit each person's response to no more than two minutes, to keep this activity short and engaging.

Day 6: Magic Pictures

Time requirement: 5 minutes for each one

This activity aims to share personal photos with each other to get to know each other on a personal level.

Ask everyone to share two photos of themselves or their families, and let them spend five minutes talking about those photos. You should encourage the rest of the class to ask questions and make some comments, to let them know more about the student who shared the picture.

Students will be looking forward to this activity because it's visually entertaining and an excellent opportunity to learn about some personal things, especially something interesting attached to others.

Added up activities for Today

Time requirement: 5 minutes for each one

The goal of this activity is to establish some kind of friendly competition between the students. It's actually a couple of games in one, but I wanted to bring them together because they all obey the same rules. You'll need a facilitator or yourself to get involved, who has the answers but doesn't participate in the game.

For each one of them, the facilitator begins with the rules, then shares the game and keeps track of the scores. Whoever gets the most points wins, simple like that.

Here are a couple of games you can choose from:

- Spot the difference (Pictures): Share two photos with your class that are identical but have some slight differences. Give everybody three minutes to find out what the total number of differences is. Then collect the final answers from all of you and ask the student who guessed the highest number to walk through the differences. When they've done, share the ones they've missed. Winners are going to get one point.

- Spot the Difference (Live Video): it is identical to the previous game. Still, it uses live video instead of photos, which will be a little more tricky, and preferably an expert in video editing. As a facilitator, turn on the video that you picked before the class and ask everyone to focus on details. Then turn it off for a minute and play another one in which you have changed some details. For example, you can shorten the video or just take some clips out of it. When you're finished, turn this video back on and ask your team members to guess what has changed. The one who is the first person to figure them out is going to get one point.

- Online Riddles & Brain Teasers: Post a riddle or brain teaser with your students and guess the answer. After they all take their turn to guess, reveal the correct answer. Students often guess the right answer by mistake based on my experiences, so ask the person to explain how they came to their conclusion. Winners who explain their answer to the question correctly get the point. The ones who just guessed and couldn't explain their answer got nothing.

- Guess the Song: it's similar to the Trivia quiz, except it uses songs instead of questions. Play the first few seconds of the single, and let the class guess the name of it. Check for "guess the album" or "old playlist" on YouTube or Spotify to get a list of famous songs. The first person who guesses the right thing gets the point. If no one can figure out the name of the album, but they recognize the artist's name, they're going to get half of a point.

- Picture: This is a condensed version of the popular game that you can play online. Your students would need to use the "Whiteboarding" feature of your collaboration tool, which allows them to use their mouse to draw on their computer. As facilitators, select a player and give them a single word (privately via chat) to draw on the screen without saying something out loud. For example, it could be "chicken" or "tree." The player will then have a maximum of 50 seconds or a minute to draw it out while everyone guesses it. The first one who gave the correct answer for the guess wins a point. Still, if the player has run out of time before having the right answer, nobody wins, and now it's the next student's turn to play it.

- Charades: This is a typical game similar to Pictionary. Instead of drawing words out, players have to act them out in front of the class. Choose a player and give them a single name (privately via chat). For example, the word may be "telescope" or "banana." Players who act should mute their microphones, so they are not able to say things out accidentally. The first person who figured it out gets the point. If the player runs out of time before anyone guesses correctly, then no one gets any points, and you pass to the next player.

Day 7: Nail It!

Time requirements per game: 10 minutes or less

Game 1

Some activities can even be just sounds without anything else. To make fun as simple as that, you can pick a sound (like a bird call or some other weird sounds), let them all make that sound at a time—one after another, until they all make the sound in rhythm ... or chaos. Either way, it's meant to create a few laughs and get everyone engaged when you want to have some fun with your classroom!

Game 2

Start your class with some music you like, and a game called "Name that Tune!" Let everyone open their meeting chat window, then you can start to play the first 5-10 seconds of the Song, the first person to type in the name of the Song wins! Do this in turn so that everyone brings a song of their own.

Tip: Choose songs from the '80s or '90s, or choose an Artist / Genre based on your students' general musical tastes (if you know about it). A big bonus of this game is that you can even make a classroom playlist as a part of the music culture when you have breaks in the middle of the class.

Game 3

Before everyone shows up to the classroom, let everybody come up with a bag of dry crackers (Saltines, Soda Crackers, etc.) and something to cover up their keyboard! One at a time, let students try to put two crackers in their mouths to whistle a tune of your choosing (Star Wars Theme, Baby Shark, etc.). This is to make enormous fun and let students laugh a lot as crackers fly out of their mouths. I've tried this with my team, and this is absolutely my favorite one!

Day 8: Threads of Fun

Time requirement: None

This one aims to keep your class connected continuously in a way that mimics natural interactions and discussions in the classroom. As mentioned earlier, one of the drawbacks of virtual classrooms is that you lose the traditional interactions that we are all used to. Many students love to send jokes, funny news, or GIFs to mimic this effect and share fun and informal updates with your virtual class via group chat or email. One downside is that this can be a disruption for some students. Others who are naughty will tend to send each other things that are not related to the class, so drawbacks like that will be needed to think through before sharing this activity with your students.

The best idea is to set up a separate "Fun Community Chat" thread other than your regular inbox for teaching materials. This can be achieved in a variety of ways. One way is to set up a separate "chat room" using your favorite group chat program (Slack or Webex Teams). Another way to use email is to create a particular mailing list with some words like "fun." For example, something like funny.updates@lol.com website shares with your students, tells them how to use it, and the specific rules to use it.

This sounds too random but actually can play a huge role. The idea is to achieve:

- Make it easy for your students to unsubscribe it, or you can cancel it as long as you need to.

- Stop sharing something significant or relevant to teaching in that thread.
- Compared to catching your students texting each other secretly but having no idea what they are talking about, this is a perfect way for you to get involved in their social activities and enhance their bond.

In that way, students can opt-out of this thread without worrying about missing any significant updates that are going on in the chat room. And it helps you redirect any off-topic discussions from regular class-related places to this thread so that you avoid interrupting everyone's workflow.

Some of the ideas you can share in that fun chat thread include:

- Funny jokes
- Interesting or educational videos on YouTube
- Dishes that nobody has tried before
- Celebrations and announcements of life events
- Simply showing off our pets and exciting places we've been to last weekend.

Again, you may want to establish some rules before you start this activity so that your students won't end up insulting anyone or playing with it rather than listening to your class. The goal is to provide a forum for them to share any updates related to the level. And please do not discuss any sensitive topics, which will also be one of the most essential rules.

Day 9: Virtual Tap

Time requirement: Just one minute to answer, several minutes to prepare

This activity aims to connect everyone in an informal group chat and enjoy some fun time. You can simply use your daily email account. Still, unlike the separate group chat we talked about, for this one, you should limit the off-topic updates to a weekly "answer all" question.

Here's how it works, on a specific day (like Friday after class or during lunch breaks) every week. You can submit a question to all of your students through email to let them reply to all and give their own answers and opinions about it. Some items may be as follows:

- What's the last book you've read?
- What is your most commonly used emoji?
- What song is that you're afraid to say that you like it?
- What's your plan for this upcoming weekend?

And here are some basic rules go with it:

- Everyone will respond within 48 hours, and if anyone fails to do it, they can no longer reply. This will encourage students to respond and limit never-ending threads.
- Everyone can reply as many two times as possible.

The benefit of this practice is that it fits well for students who live in different time zones, so recipients won't feel left out because of time lags since this is not time-sensitive at all.

Day 10: 1 plus 2

Time requirement: 5 minutes per student

This is a classic activity that can be played in a remote environment and lets them learn more about their classmates.

Here's the way to do it.

Just pick a random rest time before you start it, ask one student to share two truths and a lie about themselves, and others can do it in random order.

They should pick the facts that none of their students can easily find out within all 3 of them.
For instance:

- I have served as a part-time cook.
- I'm playing the piano.
- I'm speaking four languages.

Two of these would be true, and one of them would be a lie. Make sure the lie sounds the same as the truths to others who don't know you well (e.g., "I was the swim champion of my high school," not "I won the Olympic swimming gold medal" Or "I bought a Ferrari last week").

The goal is for each student to figure out which is the lie. After everybody's guessed, the speaker can tell them the reality. Everyone can have some discussions about things he or she just said. This game is a lot faster, and students can play it verbally without writing down anything.

Play this when it's sunny out there

Time requirement: 10 minutes or less

Whether it's a tour of their back yard or their neighborhood, give your students a chance to take others around their local areas and stretch their bodies in the middle of a long, long class. Just make sure the WiFi signal is good enough to connect with each other when walking down the street or far away from home. Simply ask them to go out of their home, and show us around (make sure to let them watch the traffic and not go too far away), introduce their favorite coffee shops, and even introduce the rest of the class to the neighbor who they come across every day. Do you all live in the same place, but in different areas? Make them share their favorite part of the area in which they live – their favorite restaurant, shop, park, etc. Give your students a glimpse into the world of each other.

Tip: As the teacher who starts this, I strongly recommend you begin by offering them a tour of your area just as a demonstration. When you do that, it's going to encourage others to do the same thing.

Day 11: The Children's Book

Time requirement: 40 minutes

This should be a great activity to improve their creativity, ability to organize new information, and teamwork skills, which can even be one of their funny projects to complete. Basically, you will break your class into two or three groups, depending on the size (the optimal group size is 3-5 students). Challenge each group to create a simple children's book or just some chapters around some topics to illustrate some aspects of their works. Let them know that the activity's goal is to practice using innovative approaches to simplify the complex.

Some examples are like below:

Life Insurance: Clarify why life insurance is essential for a 4-year-old.

Astronaut: Illustrate what an astronaut does for a 4-year-old.

Your book will not be longer than 15 pages (including the cover and back page). Everyone in their group must make a contribution, which should be written onto the cover page. After receiving all the books, they submitted, pick a student as the representative to read these stories to the rest of the class. Tell your groups don't worry about whether the final book is perfect or not. Just get it done! Also, make sure to give each group 1 hour to finish it just to be fair.

One more question for the group: Which one is your favorite book, and why?

Day 12: High and Low

Time requirement: 10 minutes

This is an excellent easy check-in question to ask after a busy week when your students just had tons of courses, just finished their exams or the completion of a big project. Start the class, go around and ask everyone to share one high (favorite moment/completion) and one low (lowest favorite moment/frustration). Ask your students questions below ...

What's the high and low for them about things below:

- Today's class?
- The events or projects from the past week?
- After the week of exams?
- Or just throughout the last weekend?

Example: "My high Today was that I have finally finished the project that I've been working on with other classmates for three weeks. My low, I accidentally missed a class last Thursday due to some personal issues".

Tip: Make a routine – pose this question at the end of each month. After a while, your students will answer the questions prepared and in a more organized way.

Tip: As an activity, leaders to host this activity, try to keep their answers short, and make more time for the discussions or solutions towards them.

Get to know some more cultures if you have an international classroom.

The purpose of this activity is to provide some really cool information and background about how your classroom is linked to various countries and cities around the world.

To play, simply share a world map with your students (either before or during the class, depends on how much time you have) and ask them to drop pins on each city or country as below:

- The city they were born in (with a blue pin)
- The city they have been to or lived in the past (using red pins)
- The city they or their parents are living in Today (using a green pin)

All of them will have their own version of the map and present it to the rest of the class. Your students will walk through where they were born, where they lived, and more details about the city and the country. When they've done, they should pick one of the places with pins, and then another student should take the turn and spend a couple of minutes talking about it. The presenter will also need to talk about something interesting about the culture or even some funny truths about some local restaurants. They can also mix it up by highlighting the "three best things to do" in that town or country. Five minutes can pass quickly, so it's best to just focus on one or two students at each time if you don't have enough time to do it or if you prefer to keep it as a daily activity.

Always stay together

Staying connected as a big family means a lot for both you and your students during this time as we do not see each other very often. "Stay Chat" is a quick check-in every 2-3 months with your students to see how things are going and whether there is something you can do to better help them.

Note, this is not a performance evaluation. Still, an intended check-in to see how the student's life, study, and daily stuff are going. Your job is to listen to them, comfort and encourage them, and find ways to help them grow and improve themselves faster.

As an example, you might say:

"I just wanted to check in to see how things were going for you. I really appreciate having you as a part of my class. You have made some progress that you should be proud of, and I wanted to make sure your life and studies have been excellent throughout the past few months. And feel free to let me know what else you want to share with me.

Possible Discussion Questions are as below:

- In general, how did things go?
- What are the things in your studies and classes that you love the most? The least of them?
- What was your greatest challenge? How can I better help you with this challenge?
- Is there any input or suggestion you'd like to send me on how we can make the classroom better?

- Any feedback you have on me or my approaches?
- Do you feel like you're learning and growing up here? If not, what do you want to know? How can I make it easier?
- Is there anything I can do to help you improve your learning and experience here in our classroom?
- How have you been getting along with others?
- What goals would you like to reach in the next 6 (12) months?

After that, agree to follow up on the actions and to the next time.

A review for the year

Any organization and community need a review for many purposes. This is an excellent opportunity for your online class to let your students reflect on how they have been, what they have been doing. It's also a perfect chance for you to give your students something unique that will have a lasting effect on your classroom's culture and success. Especially for this year, prepare this yearly review for your classroom when it comes to the end of the year.

- Choose the date, the time for the review, and invite your students through email.
- Send a list of the Reflection Questions to each student, and encourage them to add something

on there if they feel necessary and would like to share.

- Set the tone of the review session by presenting its intention and the procedure to go with.
- Go through the shared list together and enjoy all the shared information, the laughs, the development, and learnings. You should also expect to set some milestones and give your reviews.

An example will be like this:

"Today, we're going to take a few hours to pause and reflect back on this year. Most of the time, we're so busy studying and learning that it's hard to recall what happened last week, let alone what happened months ago. When we get busy, we appear to hurry from a project to another, from one class to another, especially sometimes when we are going through main milestones, getting ourselves busy preparing for many courses, exams, presentations, and lessons. Today, It's about taking the time to just present and reflect on what has been achieved and what is still left over, set some plans, then celebrate how much we've grown up and as a big family over the last year.

Questions for their reflections:

- What significant events/changes/challenges have you encountered over this year?
- What talents, skillsets, or abilities have you gained or gained during this year?
- What have you learned to conquer those challenges?

- What important lessons did we learn as a family?
- How did we develop together so far this year?
- What made you proud of yourself and for us this year?
- What are you most thankful for looking back on this year as part of this family?

Day 13: Customer Talk

Time requirement per option: 30 Minute

This can be an excellent activity for your college students, to get them prepared for a future job, as in the future we will need to speak with our customers and deal with some tricky situations, whether they can do it well with some past experiences, or just try to do it for the first time, it's always beneficial to practice this as they are getting there soon.

Option 1

Have each student write a challenging customer scenario they've dealt with personally or heard others dealing with before. Let them write that all down and send over to you. Once you review and compile them together, get the whole class together online. Next, you will designate a student who will act as a customer and then assign the customer service representative's role to another student. Pick up and present one of the scenarios to the whole class, give the two "actors" five minutes to read through, and prepare to act on the same situation. It might sound a bit more challenging to the "customer representative," besides laughing, you all need to come up with some alternative thinking and suggestions to move forward. This will be an excellent opportunity for the whole class to learn about since customer service is always a vital part of any company they will work for in the future.

Option 2

Some things can help companies improve their services or products, such as taking time to think of and understand user experiences. This can be a severe activity and fun and helpful. You can Invite a student from another class to attend one of your virtual courses, or you can let some of your students conduct interviews with others who are outside your class and get some feedback to share with others.

Here are some templates for your students to send to others. They can send it to other students, staff, or even your colleagues, to practice. As the interview request, they are not really working for a company and don't have any products. So this is just a practice and let them use their imaginations and focus on practicing their words.

Dear Mary,

This is John from ABC Inc. I hope this message will find you doing well. How's the family doing? My team and I are always searching for ways to provide more service to the students we represent. This week and next, everyone on our team will be interviewing our clients in several groups, so if you're available, I'd love to have the opportunity to interview you. I know you're busy, but if you could spare 5-10 minutes, I'd love to hear your thoughts to better understand your experience with our services. If you don't have the time, I fully understand that, and we can talk about it later on. Let me know if you're going to be available for a short call.

Sincerely,
John

Hi Mike, this is John from ABC Inc.

Thank you for agreeing to make a short call with me Today. How were you? As I mentioned in the previous email, the call aims to learn about your experience. I have some questions here for you if you don't mind answering?

Here are some examples you can use:

- Why did you want to engage with our services at the beginning?

- Why did you choose to keep going with us?

- What's your favorite thing about working with us and our products?

- What do you think we can do to take your customer experience to the next level?

- Is there anything else you would like to mention?

Option 3

Here is the assignment that you can send to your students to complete for practicing customer service:

At the end of our class today, I would like everyone to pretend that you are a customer who is using or trying your products or services. That customer could even be a potential employee who is considering working for your company). So I would like you to search for information that you think you would like to include in the introduction and presentation. Then organize your language to talk about your products and make you a great company in the market. What do you think about that? What do you think consumers will see or hear for the first time? Take a few screenshots and get ready for our next class to discuss. The goal is to come up with one easy thing you should do to boost your online experience.

In your next meeting, let's share your findings and thoughts and ideas for improvement, and if it would make a difference.

Day 14: Virtual Clubs

Time requirement per club: 1 hour / day
'

Club 1

Book club: Organize a virtual book club with your students or even include their friends. Select a book or article with your students together. If you all have something you like in common, you can let them read and discuss their feelings after reading the book. You may also want to purchase a digital copy of the book or article for your students and then arrange a meeting for everyone to come back together and talk about the book.

Movie Club as an option: No readings, no problems, try a movie club, or even a podcast club!

Club 2

Training club: Mary has always done excellent math exams, Lucy is a master of Excel, Dave does well in writing and music class, Luis is a physics...etc. You've got such a wealth of knowledge and expertise in your lesson. Why don't you scale up to better use it? Invite your students to have a mini virtual training session with their classmates. Ask Mary if she'd be open to hosting a mini-training session and sharing her philosophy and approaches to challenging math problems. And if she is free to let Lucy teach some unique skills in handling tasks in Excel. Not only do students learn from each other, but you recognize your students in such a way by giving them the chance to share their skills and success.

Club 3

Infuse a little playful rivalry by organizing a trivia contest. You can either make this a one-off event during a class or an ongoing competition where you ask a question at the end of each call. Either way, divide your students into two or three teams and let the competition begin. Make up your own question or do a quick search for "trivia questions," and you'll have thousands of options to choose from. Pouring more motivations by setting up a winner's prize!

Day 15: Time for Coffee!

Time Required: Approx. 15 minutes

Just to connect all the students in your class regularly, you can choose lunchtime or late afternoons. Again, make sure to pick the right time if you have students living in different time zones. You can encourage everyone to have a quick chat with their favorite cup of coffee or tea. You can even encourage everyone to bring their favorite food.

The idea is to keep this open as an optional live forum that encourages the students to join and just chat about everything. The only rule is that the chat only allows anything but related to their classes, projects, or exams. It can be something random, funny, and life-oriented to keep your students excited about it.

This is a low maintenance activity because your students don't need to mentally prepare for it. They usually have coffee, snacks, or dessert during lunchtime or late afternoon anyway. They just need to show up there, sharing and chatting if they like to. Some of them want to talk about a show on Netflix or a new book they've been reading. Others like to talk about the latest news.

Just make sure to set it as a routine activity, and put some time limitation to it as 15min or so.

Day 16: Mi Familia!

The purpose of this activity is for your students to show up with their family members, pets, or friends. It is crucial to create a harmonious and surrounded environment for all of us, getting to know each other better, along with each other's family members.

It is an online version of "bring your family to work" day. It is an excellent way for students and their family members to chat around, communicate, and have some fun. The connection with others is essential, particularly during a pandemic when everyone is locked at home and missing their social interactions.

This also gives their family members more understanding about their performances, friends, and what kind of an online class they are studying in. Bringing other family members with them also means getting more laughs and funny stories behind themselves.

During the call, make sure to control the conversation flow to prevent crosstalk (because it can get really crazy with some little kids and pets around other than their parents). You can remind everyone to have no more than six minutes to their updates just to get everyone involved. To facilitate the discussion, ask each student to spend the first three minutes on their family members' introductions. They can talk about whatever is interesting in their lives for the rest of the 3 minutes.

This is also a perfect opportunity for their family members to say hello and chat about things they love doing. They can even speak about some exciting habits that students never talk about during their classes. My experience always ends up being tons of laughs and jokes, and the professor's voice of "time is up!".

Day 17: Virtual Workout

Time requirement: Approximately. 15 minutes

The purpose of this activity is to remind your students to concentrate on their physical well-being and personal health. It is on top of everything, especially if they don't have enough exercise.

It may seem a little awkward for your students to do a workout in the middle of the day. You can certainly put it in the early morning. This is an activity that a lot of students will enjoy during the coronavirus lockout. Most of them will start to realize they need to make sure they are in good shape and good health, which keeps them strong and healthy.

Note: It's a good idea to consult with their parents before you carry out this operation. There might be some students with special conditions who need to be taken care of.

The easiest way to do a team workout is to consult someone from your class who has a fitness coach or who is good at doing this in their family or network. You will always manage to find one. Give everyone a simple 15-minute walkthrough on basic principles of workouts. An alternative is to invite a qualified fitness instructor to join your video call and lead all of you through with some expert advice.

If none of these options is working, you can play a short free YouTube video and let everyone participate and follow through. Try several videos to see which one fits the best for your students.

And make sure to remind everyone to wear comfortable clothes and clear a small area in their room before they start to work out.

Day 18: Be Mindful

Time requirement per mode: 10-15 minutes

Mode 1

During some busy time, your students sometimes jump into a new class, with half of them still trying to process information from the previous class they just came from. Consider starting your course with a 2-minute mindful transition. As soon as students enter the meeting, you will say, "Let's take a few minutes to make the transition to our current class."

Next, allow students no more than 3 minutes to take notes of any thoughts or follow-up actions from their previous class so that they can be fully prepared and present at this new class.

Second, you shall ask them to take 3-5 deep breaths together, to put anything else down, for this new environment.

Third, let's get started!

Mode 2

Research has found that students who take 5-10 minutes to write down 3-5 things that they're grateful for at the beginning or end of their day are 100 percent happier than those who do not have this habit! Why? What we're focused on is what we don't have and what we are trying to get. If we take time to see what is good about what we already had, we will be able to see ourselves and the world around us in a much better way and be full of hope!

Start a class appreciation exercise by the beginning of the end of your virtual class by letting everyone write 3-5 things for which they are grateful. And let them share their contents. All others shall give some encouragement and motivation. Try doing it for 20 days and see how it impacts you and your students' lives positively!

Mode 3

Start a class appreciation exercise by starting "Happy Friday" or "Thankful Thursday." Post a question by email or text message every week and ask your students to reflect. Answer the questions yourself first to help inspire others to do the same thing. Here are 12 questions to help you get started:

- What did I learn recently that helped me grow?
- What are the opportunities I have right now that I'm grateful for?
- What physical skills do I have yet to take for granted?
- What kind of material possessions am I grateful for, and why?
- What did I see Today or in the last month that was inspired?
- Who can I see every day at my class, and whom do I see the most amount of time?
- Who's the one that I'm so glad I get to work with, and why?

- Who's the one in the classroom that helped me the most amount of the time?
- What I'm particularly grateful for studying here with all of you, and why?
- What other things are going on in your life that you are grateful for, and why?
- Who's the person I don't speak to very much in a day, but if I lost them tomorrow, it would be devastating? (Take this as a hint to reach out Today!)
- In what way did I get better now than I was a year ago?

Support your community

This activity aims to have your students get involved in helping their local communities. They would need to spend a little on this activity, so this is not mandatory for everyone.

Many small businesses have been struggling to survive the pandemic. This activity would inspire your students to support the students around them by giving back.

In the week before the activity, you should give everyone a budget (let's say $50 for each person) and ask them to spend the money on something relevant to their local community.

Here are a few ideas about where to spend the money:

- local bakery cookies
- online music lessons at the nearby music school

- supermarket stores from a limited foreign market
- Car parts from the local mechanic
- The food at the nearby restaurant

Once they have all finished, during the class, you should ask each of them to spend a few minutes talking about:

- What they were purchasing
- The history of the local business
- Why did they support it, and what it means to them

Doing so will help the class share what is most important to them individually and offer others ideas about sharing and helping others that they haven't considered.

An alternative to purchasing goods or services is to buy gift cards if holiday seasons are coming. Gift cards give companies the cash flow they need to help support themselves in a tough time.

Day 19: A Little Gratitude

Time requirement per mode: None

Mode 1

Every day we are moving forward, achieving lots of progress in our virtual classroom, thanks to all others' help. It would be impressive to show some appreciation to others whom you saw have helped you a lot. You always want to say thank you but never get a chance. Just imagine that they will never forget that when they receive a video from you that shows your appreciation, enhancing your bond with each other down the road. It doesn't have to be super long, just a simple 15-20 second video. Combine all the videos into a short file, even pair a song with it, and surprise them in your next meeting. I guarantee they're never going to forget it!

Mode 2

It's also important to express your appreciation daily. It doesn't have to be said whenever someone just helped you. Simply say thank you to everyone you are with. Ask your students to take 5 minutes before each virtual class to show their appreciation for the students around them.

Mode 3

Just because you can't drop a hand-written note on another's desk doesn't mean you need to go back to send an impersonal e-card! A hand-written card is always more important than an email because the person has spent time writing down their words and took the time to deliver it. When you want to make your message a bit more meaningful, just spend five minutes writing down your message on a card, a piece of paper, or even a sticky note. Even if we are learning and teaching at home, we can still take a screenshot of the card and send it to the person with a message saying, "The next time I see you, I'm going to give you a hard copy, thank you! "Want to take a step further? Record your message of thanks in a video and send it to them. You are assured of having a day!

Don't you know what to say? Below are a couple of ideas to get you going.

- Thank you for always pushing for us to try new things.

- Thank you for always keeping us safe.

- Thank you for always keeping our classroom clean 365 days a year.

- Thank you for remembering our birthdays all the time.

- Thank you for always getting up earlier to prepare meals.

- Thank you for sharing informative posts and activities.

- Thank you for getting your projects done on time.

- Thank you for always reminding us that we should collaborate with others.

- Thank you very much for putting up with my craziness.

- Thank you for answering the same question many times when I'm being annoyed.

Day 20: One Thing

Time Available: Approximately 30 minutes

The purpose of a class is for everyone to enter the video conference. The meaning is to gather around and learn from the teacher, and check-in sees if everyone is doing great, and get an update from the rest of the class on what's going well and not OK. Besides, everyone can share a personal statement about themselves or their lives, especially if they are super excited about it.

Here is how here practice works:

You will need to set aside thirty minutes for a weekly "video roundtable." It is not a comprehensive meeting to cover many learning materials, but instead a general overview of how things are going with them, on both their lives and studies.

There are two keys to the functioning of this activity. First, give everyone some heads up ahead of time. It is essential for all to have some preparations, instead of just jumping into their calendars without notifications, getting them rushed on this. Second, every student needs to be involved. That way, you're going to make sure everyone's camera and the mood are ready when they enter the room, and they're prepared to share their updates with each other.

To add some structure to this, you can let them answer the three questions ahead of their sharings:

1. What's one thing that's been going really well lately with you?

2. What's one thing that you have been working on?

3. What's one major thing that's been going on with you personally, anything you are excited about?

Some types of answers can be as below:

1. We're doing well with the new project you assigned two weeks ago — we've completed it ahead of time, and we are pleased about our progress. And by the way, a huge thank you to Mike for helping us out last week.

2. One thing we should do better is to be a little more open to some help from other groups, as they will give us some useful perspectives as a third party

3. A personal note is that I'm going to take a week off beginning next Friday. I will spend the time with my parents. We're going to spend a couple of days on the East Coast. And we have been looking forward to it for quite a long time.

The focus should be on the person talking. Other students of the class are welcome to ask or comment on anything they are interested in to feel like an open forum. Also, make sure to have the video turned on, which is essential to read students' facial and body expressions as they are speaking. It can make you feel like you're all sitting in a meeting room together.

THANK YOU!

Congratulations on getting through this whole 20-day challenge. You could have picked from dozens of books on online teaching, but you took a chance and checked out this one. We believe you've made a great choice!

If you find this book helpful, please take a moment, leave a review, and share it with your colleagues, your students, and friends. Your suggestions and satisfaction are the greatest motivation for our efforts now and in the future.

We feel honored to have put our best efforts to support you and your online classroom on this incredible journey!